WORKBOOK FOR

The ESL Writer's Handbook

Janine Carlock
Maeve Eberhardt
Jaime Horst
Lionel Menasche

Pitt Series in ESL
University of Michigan Press

ISBN-13: 978-0-472-03404-8

2013   2012   4   3   2

CONTENTS

SECTION 1. THE WRITING PROCESS   **1**

UNDERSTANDING WRITING ASSIGNMENTS [*Handbook*, Section 1B]   **2**

1.1   Key Words in Writing Prompts   2
1.2   Identifying Key Words in Writing Assignments   3

GENERATING IDEAS [*Handbook*, Section 1D]   **4**

1.3   Brainstorming   4
1.4   Discussion (Pair or Group Brainstorming)   5
1.5   Journalistic Questions   6
1.6   Freewriting (Writing without Stopping)   7
1.7   Listing   8
1.8   Outlining   9
1.9   Visual Mapping (Clustering)   10
1.10   Generating Ideas: Review   11

SECTION 2. ESSAY STRUCTURE   **13**

SHAPING A PARAGRAPH [*Handbook*, Section 2A]   **14**

2.1   Topic and Perspective   14
2.2   Finding a Topic Sentence in a Paragraph   15
2.3   Writing Topic Sentences   16
2.4   Writing a Topic Sentence for a Paragraph   17

SHAPING AN ESSAY [*Handbook*, Section 2B]   **18**

2.5   Essay Introduction   18
2.6   Essay Conclusion   19
2.7   Essay Introduction and Conclusion   20
2.8   Description   21
2.9   Simple Definition   22
2.10   Complex Definition   23
2.11   Examples   24
2.12   Paragraph Unity   25
2.13   Creating Paragraph Coherence   26
2.14   Paragraph Coherence   27
2.15   Using Transitions for Coherence in a Paragraph   28
2.16   Using Transitions for Coherence in an Essay   29

SECTION 3. PATTERNS OF ESSAY ORGANIZATION   31

NARRATIVE ESSAY [*Handbook*, Section 3A]   32
3.1 Ordering a Narrative Paragraph   32
3.2 Practice with *When* and *While*   33

PROCESS ESSAY [*Handbook*, Section 3B]   34
3.3 Practice with Process Words and Phrases   34
3.4 Connecting Ideas Using Process Words and Phrases   35

COMPARISON/CONTRAST ESSAY [*Handbook*, Section 3C]   36
3.5 Connecting Ideas Using Comparison/Contrast Words and Phrases 36
3.6 Using Comparison/Contrast Words to Create a Paragraph   37

CAUSE-AND-EFFECT ESSAY [*Handbook*, Section 3D]   38
3.7 Identifying Cause-and-Effect Words and Phrases   38
3.8 Connecting Ideas Using Cause-and-Effect Words and Phrases 40

ARGUMENT ESSAY [*Handbook*, Section 3E]   41
3.9 Identifying Argument Words and Phrases   41
3.10 Connecting Ideas Using Logical Argument   43
3.11 Making Generalizations   44

SECTION 4. RESEARCH PAPER   45

SUMMARIZING, PARAPHRASING, AND USING QUOTATIONS [*Handbook*, Section 4D]   46
4.1 Summarizing   46
4.2 Recognizing Plagiarism   48

OUTLINING [*Handbook*, Section 4E]   51
4.3 Ordering Outline Headings   51

THESIS STATEMENTS [*Handbook*, Section 4F]   52
4.4 Thesis Statements: Argument or Report   52

APA STYLE [*Handbook*, Section 4J]   53
4.5 APA References   53

MLA STYLE [*Handbook*, Section 4K]   56
4.6 MLA Works Cited   56

SECTION 5. GRAMMAR AND STYLE   59

At Word Level

WORD FORM [*Handbook,* Section 5A]   60
5.1   Word Form   60

ARTICLES [*Handbook,* Section 5B]   61
5.2   Articles   61
5.3   Looking at Nouns in Context to Determine Article Use   62

PREPOSITIONS [*Handbook,* Section 5C]   63
5.4   Prepositions   63
5.5   Phrasal Verbs   64

WORD CHOICE IN FORMAL WRITING STYLE [*Handbook,* Section 5D]   65
5.6   Word Choice   65

REFERENCE WORDS [*Handbook,* Section 5E]   66
5.7   Reference Words   66

REDUCING WORDINESS [*Handbook,* Section 5F]   67
5.8   Reducing Wordiness in Sentences   67
5.9   Reducing Wordiness in a Paragraph   68

At Sentence Level

SUBJECT-VERB AGREEMENT [*Handbook,* Section 5H]   69
5.10 Subject-Verb Agreement   69

RUN-ON SENTENCES AND SENTENCE FRAGMENTS [*Handbook,* Section 5I]   70
5.11 Fragments   70
5.12 Run Ons and Fragments   71

COMMA SPLICE [*Handbook,* Section 5J]   72
5.13 Comma Splices   72

RELATIVE CLAUSES: RESTRICTIVE AND NON-RESTRICTIVE [*Handbook,* Section 5K]   73
5.14 Comma Use in Relative Clauses   73

PARALLEL STRUCTURE [*Handbook,* Section 5L]   74
5.15 Parallel Structure   74

SENTENCE COMBINING [*Handbook,* Section 5M]   75
5.16 Combining Sentences   75
5.17 Using Specific Structures to Revise Sentences   77

SENTENCE VARIETY [*Handbook,* Section 5N]   78
5.18 Creating More Variety in Sentence Structure   78

SECTION 6. PUNCTUATION — 79

PERIOD [*Handbook*, Section 6A] — 80
6.1   Period at End of Sentence: Run On — 80
6.2   Period at End of Sentence: Correcting Errors — 81
6.3   Period with Decimals — 82

QUESTION MARK [*Handbook*, Section 6B] — 83
6.4   Question Mark and Period — 83

EXCLAMATION POINT [*Handbook*, Section 6C] — 84
6.5   Exclamation Point for Strong Feeling — 84
6.6   Exclamation Points, Periods, or Question Marks in a Conversation — 85

COMMA [*Handbook*, Section 6D] — 86
6.7   Comma after Introductory or Transitional Words and Phrases — 86
6.8   Comma after Introductory Clause — 87
6.9   Comma before Conjunctions Linking Independent Clauses — 88
6.10 Comma with Lists of Words, Phrases, or Clauses — 89
6.11 Comma with Coordinate Adjectives — 90
6.12 Comma with Quotations — 91
6.13 Comma with Abbreviations — 92
6.14 Comma with Contrasting or Interrupting Expressions or Those Needing Separation for Clarity — 93

SEMICOLON [*Handbook*, Section 6E] — 94
6.15 Semicolon with Independent Clauses — 94
6.16 Semicolon — 95

COLON [*Handbook*, Section 6F] — 96
6.17 Colon — 96

SECTION 1
THE WRITING PROCESS

Understanding Writing Assignments

Generating Ideas

1

Understanding Writing Assignments
[*Handbook,* Section 1B, pages 7–10]

Exercise 1.1: Key Words in Writing Prompts

Match each key word with its definition. Write the letter of the definition next to the word in the space provided.

Group A

1. ____ *summarize*
2. ____ *describe*
3. ____ *narrate*
4. ____ *illustrate*
5. ____ *contrast*
6. ____ *evaluate*

a. give examples or an extended example
b. describe dissimilarities
c. provide the main points only, with no details
d. provide general statements and details that present a clear idea
e. explain the strong and weak points and give your opinion
f. tell the story of some events

Group B

1. ____ *challenge*
2. ____ *assess*
3. ____ *prove*
4. ____ *define*
5. ____ *compare*
6. ____ *review*

a. describe similarities and differences
b. present and discuss the weak points of an argument or explanation
c. describe the general class to which a thing belongs and how it differs from all others in that class
d. explain why something is true
e. give a description of the issues involved
f. give a carefully thought-out judgment on something

Group C

1. ____ *outline*
2. ____ *enumerate*
3. ____ *address*
4. ____ *relate*
5. ____ *clarify*
6. ____ *trace*

a. explain the connections between two or more items
b. deal with, consider, discuss
c. provide a description that focuses only on main ideas, with no details
d. describe a series of events in sequence
e. give a descriptive list
f. explain in a way that makes the ideas easy to understand

Group D

1. ____ *explain*
2. ____ *interpret*
3. ____ *support*
4. ____ *defend*
5. ____ *list*

a. present facts to show that an explanation is true
b. provide information to make an issue clear
c. explain the meaning
d. give arguments to support a position or claim against criticism
e. provide a series of items

Group E

1. ____ *justify*
2. ____ *discuss*
3. ____ *state*
4. ____ *criticize*
5. ____ *process*

a. say what something is
b. something done in steps or stages
c. consider all aspects of an issue
d. give reasons for doing or saying something
e. evaluate the strong and weak points

Exercise 1.2: Identifying Key Words in Writing Assignments

Underline the key words in each writing assignment.

1. Discuss this proposition: All cultural and arts events and sites, such as libraries, concerts, museums, and festivals, should be made available to the public free or at little cost. Defend your position with facts and examples.

2. Describe the process of photosynthesis. Provide diagrams to support your explanation.

3. Trace the history of the roles of women and men in your country. Address economic and social aspects, and discuss changes that have occurred over the past century.

4. Compare two of the great revolutions in world history. Evaluate the reasons behind and the results of each revolution.

5. Assess the benefits and drawbacks of attending a university in a foreign country. Enumerate at least three issues that a student should or should not consider when choosing to study abroad, and support your opinion with examples and personal anecdotes.

Generating Ideas
[*Handbook,* Section 1D, pages 12–18]

Exercise 1.3: Brainstorming

Brainstorm on one of these topics. Write your ideas in the space provided. Answers will vary.

1. travel

2. popular music

3. taking risks

Workbook for The ESL Writer's Handbook
Janine Carlock, Maeve Eberhardt, Lionel Menasche, Jamie Horst
http://www.press.umich.edu/titleDetailDesc.do?id=1247278
Michigan ELT, 2010

WORKBOOK ANSWER KEY

Section 1. The Writing Process

Understanding Writing Assignments

Exercise 1.1: Key Words in Writing Prompts (page 2)

	1.	2.	3.	4.	5.	6.
Group A	c	d	f	a	b	e
Group B	b	f	d	c	a	e
Group C	c	e	b	a	f	d
Group D	b	c	a	d	e	
Group E	d	c	a	e	b	

Exercise 1.2: Identifying Key Words in Writing Assignments (page 3)

1. <u>Discuss</u> the following proposition: All cultural and arts events and sites, such as libraries, concerts, museums, and festivals, should be made available to the public free or at little cost. <u>Defend</u> your position with facts and examples.
2. <u>Describe</u> the process of photosynthesis. <u>Provide</u> diagrams to <u>support</u> your explanation.
3. <u>Trace</u> the history of the roles of women and men in your country. <u>Address</u> economic and social aspects, and <u>discuss</u> changes that have occurred over the past century.
4. <u>Compare</u> two of the great revolutions in world history. <u>Evaluate</u> the reasons behind and the results of each revolution.
5. <u>Assess</u> the benefits and drawbacks of attending a university in a foreign country. <u>Enumerate</u> at least three issues that a student should or should not consider when choosing to study abroad, and <u>support</u> your opinion with examples and personal anecdotes.

Generating Ideas

Exercises 1.3 to 1.10 (pages 4–11)
Answers will vary.

Section 2. Essay Structure

Shaping a Paragraph

Exercise 2.1: Topic and Perspective (page 14)

1. (My writing habits) <u>changed after taking the writing course</u>.
2. <u>There should not be</u> (mandatory curricula for young children).
3. Although both (Shanghai and Hong Kong) are cities in China, <u>many cultural differences exist between them</u>.
4. <u>Parents should take responsibility</u> for (teaching their children how to behave) and <u>keep them quiet</u>, especially in a public environment.
5. An (excess of watching television) can have <u>harmful effects on children</u>.

Exercise 1.4: Discussion (Pair or Group Brainstorming)

With a partner or a small group, discuss one of these topics. Write some new ideas generated by your discussion in the space provided. Answers will vary.

1. Having practical experience is better than knowing theory.

2. National voluntary or military service should be required of all young people.

Exercise 1.5: Journalistic Questions

Apply the journalistic questions (the *Wh-* words: *Who? When? Where? Why? What? How?*) to one of these topics. Write responses to each question in the space provided. Answers will vary.

1. Internet addiction

2. English as a global language

Exercise 1.6: Freewriting (Writing without Stopping)

Choose one of these topics. Freewrite for three minutes in the space provided. Then underline some ideas from your freewriting that might be important to include in an essay on the chosen topic. Answers will vary.

1. Leisure is important for students.

2. Learning never ends.

Exercise 1.7: Listing

Select one of these topics. Then list some ideas related to that topic in the space provided.
Answers will vary.

1. rural vs. urban life

2. characteristics of a good leader

Exercise 1.8: Outlining

Choose one of these topics. Develop your ideas in an outline form by listing your main ideas and then adding more specific ideas under the main headings. Write your outline in the space provided. Answers will vary

1. riding a bicycle safely

2. types of popular music

3. traditional holidays and festivals

4. choosing a field of study

5. the importance of studying history

6. electronic devices

Exercise 1.9: Visual Mapping (Clustering)

Choose one of these topics. Create a visual map to generate ideas about it. Diagram your map in the space provided. Answers will vary.

1. success

2. space exploration

3. politics

4. medicine

Exercise 1.10: Generating Ideas: Review

Choose one of the topics listed in *Workbook Exercise 1.2: Identifying Key Words in Writing Assignments* (page 3), and generate ideas about it as if you are planning to write an essay. Use one or more of the idea-generating techniques to develop your ideas: brainstorming, discussion, journalistic questions, freewriting, listing, outlining, or visual mapping. Write your ideas in the space provided. Answers will vary.

SECTION 2
ESSAY STRUCTURE

Shaping a Paragraph

Shaping an Essay

Shaping a Paragraph
[*Handbook,* Section 2A, pages 20–22]

Exercise 2.1: Topic and Perspective

Circle the topic, and underline the perspective in each topic sentence.

1. My writing habits changed after taking the writing course.

2. There should not be mandatory curricula for young children.

3. Although both Shanghai and Hong Kong are cities in China, many cultural differences exist between them.

4. Parents should take responsibility for teaching their children how to behave and keep them quiet, especially in a public environment.

5. An excess of watching television can have harmful effects on children.

Exercise 2.2: Finding a Topic Sentence in a Paragraph

Underline the topic sentence in the paragraph.

Paper, one of the most commonly used materials in daily life, is made from trees, a resource that can easily be exhausted on the earth. Generally, after using paper, people just throw it away. It takes 30 to 50 years to grow a tree, but the time we take to use paper and throw it away can be just a few minutes. We cannot grow trees as fast as we exhaust them. As a result, too many of the world's trees will be destroyed unless we find good ways to deal with the used paper. Trees also reduce the content of carbon dioxide in the air and improve the environment. Therefore, we should recycle used paper products as much as we can in order to save trees for other uses and have a better environment as well.

Exercise 2.3: Writing Topic Sentences

Write a possible topic sentence for each paragraph. Answers may vary.

1. _____

   _____

   First of all, sports can make people healthy, compared to playing computer games, playing cards, and so on. When you do fitness exercises, you can strengthen your body. When you swim, you can improve your flexibility. In addition, sports can make people more cooperative. For instance, in a soccer team, eleven people play together. The teammates need to cooperate with each other in order to win the match. If someone just wants to show off, the rate of success of the team will decrease.

2. _____

   _____

   When you are using a credit card, you are borrowing money from the credit card company. You can repay it when you want, but you also have to pay the interest. However, when you are using a debit card, you are using the money that is actually in your account. You are not allowed to overdraw, which means that you are not borrowing any money, and you do not need to pay any interest. Through a comparison, we find that debit cards have the benefits of credit cards, like convenience and safety, without the disadvantages of credit cards, namely, debt. In short, I suggest that the use of credit cards should be discouraged, and debit cards should be encouraged.

3. _____

   _____

   Every community has its own cultural values that influence the lives and thoughts of the individuals living in that community. As part of my own community, I was influenced by certain social principles that contributed to shaping my life and choosing a specific major in my studies, disability and communication disorders. In addition, from my early childhood, I was taught by my parents to respect older people and help them, especially those who suffer from any kind of disability that could hinder certain aspects of their lives.

Exercise 2.4: Writing a Topic Sentence for a Paragraph

Write a possible topic sentence for the paragraph from an essay written by a student. Where would you place it? Explain your answer. Write your sentence and explanation in the space provided.

My parents used to always point out that helping people is a humane goal that is easy to understand but hard to fulfill. They used to stress the fact that helping people purifies the spirit and gets it used to good deeds. Actually, I know of a very revealing event related to this philosophy. It occurred to a friend of mine. One day, that friend was heading to my home for a visit. On his way, he encountered an old lady who had lost her money because a robber stole her wallet. She needed to take a taxi, and she had no money with her. So she asked my friend for help. My friend also had no money with him. He brought her with him to my place, borrowed some money from me, and then handed it to the lady. Two days later, my friend came back to visit me again and told me a strange event which had happened to him. He said that on the day when he helped that lady, he went home. When he got there, his mother told him that, on her way back home, she had lost her wallet somewhere, but fortunately there was somebody who handed her money to get back home. The amount of money was exactly the same as what my friend had given to help the old lady!

Your sentence: _____

_____

Shaping an Essay
[*Handbook,* Section 2B, pages 22–51]

Exercise 2.5: Essay Introduction

Read this introductory paragraph of an essay written by a student. Then answer the questions in the space provided.

> There has always been a strong argument about human nature. Some say we are born evil and others say we are born benevolent. It seems that this is an argument without a definite answer. However, I would say absolutely that human nature is gracious. I think such a view is very important in my life because it has encouraged me to do volunteer work and has led me to study education and pursue it as my career. Also, what is more important is that it has enabled me to live happily and optimistically.

1. What do you think is the main idea of the whole essay?

2. What are the main supporting ideas that you expect will be discussed in the body of the essay?

3. In what order do you think the supporting ideas will be discussed?

Exercise 2.6: Essay Conclusion

Read the concluding paragraph in an essay written by a student. Then answer the questions in the space provided.

> To sum up, I cannot deny that giving college credits is a way to encourage students to be volunteers, and some might be inspired during their work. However, we should realize that there are great differences between the whole-hearted type and the half-hearted type discussed. The former enjoy their volunteer work, and it could have a good effect on them. On the other hand, the latter tend to be impatient and feel annoyed easily. The work could have a bad effect on them, and they may do the work badly. Thus, even if our society encourages students to work as volunteers for college credits, it will not cause them all to become more gracious and helpful in the long run because volunteer work is not something easy that needs only one's time. Instead, it is a job that needs one's heart.

1. Based on this concluding paragraph, what do you think is the main idea of the whole essay?

2. Based on this concluding paragraph, what are the main supporting ideas that you expect were discussed in the body of the essay?

3. In what order do you think the supporting ideas were discussed?

Exercise 2.7: Essay Introduction and Conclusion

1. Underline the thesis statement of the essay in the introductory paragraph.
2. Note the map (or foreshadowing) in the paragraph, and list what you expect the main points of the essay will be.
3. Underline the restatement of the thesis in the concluding paragraph.

Introduction

A friend for me is a person whom I can trust and whom I can count on in different places and in different moments. Since about 1980, I can identify three distinct periods in my life in terms of my social environment and friendships. The first period started at the beginning of my elementary school and ended when I finished high school; the second started with my undergraduate studies and ended with my Master thesis; the last one began with my PhD studies in August 2002 and continues up to now. During all these periods of my life, I met different kinds of people and I made a lot of friends who were quite important to me.

Conclusion

What I can conclude from this is that during all the time I have been a student, I have made many friends who have been a significant part of my life. I am convinced that nobody can live without friends. Certainly, if I hadn't made all these friends I would be a very different person today. In each stage of life, it is important to have people you can count on and who will help you on your journey through new challenges and experiences.

2. Main points expected:

_____

_____

_____

_____

Exercise 2.8: Description

Using descriptive language, write a brief paragraph (three to five sentences) on one of these topics. Answers will vary. Write your paragraph in the space provided.

1. a teacher or role model that you remember from your childhood

2. a favorite song, musical composition, play, or movie

3. a beautiful or memorable place that you have visited

4. the process of making your favorite meal or dish

Exercise 2.9: Simple Definition

Write a simple definition for each word. Answers will vary.

1. bus_____

_____

2. mouse_____

_____

3. banana_____

_____

Exercise 2.10: Complex Definition

Write a complex definition (one brief paragraph) for each word. Answers will vary. Write your definitions in the space provided.

1. language

2. home

3. rice

Exercise 2.11: Examples

Find the sentence in the paragraph that needs an example or detail as support. Create a logical example, and place it in the paragraph after that sentence. Write your example in the space provided, and use arrows to show where in the paragraph you would place it.

Pacer Construction Company has demonstrated strong performance on past projects and has built a good reputation among its clients. Pacer has finished all of its projects with good quality and on schedule, while often ending up under budget. That is why a large number of its clients are highly satisfied with Pacer's performance and the company has received numerous awards for its work. This recognition for its work directly reflects Pacer's work performance and the good reputation that it has built over four decades of construction experience.

Exercise 2.12: Paragraph Unity

This paragraph lacks unity because some sentences are not related to the topic. Make the paragraph more unified by removing the sentences or phrases that are not related to the main idea of the paragraph. Write the numbers of the deleted sentences in the space provided. [Sentences are numbered only for reference in this exercise.]

① Diabetes can be divided into two categories. ② One is Insulin-Dependent Diabetes (IDDs, Type I diabetes) and the other is Non–Insulin Dependent Diabetes (NIDDs, Type II diabetes). ③ It is likely that everyone knows someone who has diabetes. ④ Both types of diabetes greatly increase a person's risk for a range of serious conditions such as blindness and kidney failure. ⑤ Thus it is important to have a good relationship with one's doctor. ⑥ Older people tend to have a wide range of health issues, including breathing difficulties, heart conditions, and circulatory problems. ⑦ Moreover, diabetics can have critical risk factors for heart disease, stroke, and leg amputations. ⑧ Although both types of diabetes are related with excess glucose concentration in blood, each has its own distinguished characteristics in causes, symptoms, and treatments. ⑨ Maintaining one's health can be quite expensive, especially when one must deal with serious health problems such as diabetes.

Sentences deleted to improve unity (write the sentence numbers):

Exercise 2.13: Creating Paragraph Coherence

The sentences of this paragraph, written by a student, have been moved out of their original order. Rearrange the order of sentences to create a coherent paragraph. Write the new coherent paragraph in the space provided. More than one order is possible. [Sentences are numbered only for reference in this exercise.]

① Overall, the wine and champagne industries are very significant to the economic health of my hometown. ② Once a year the people in the rural areas harvest those grapes and sell them to companies that make several kinds of wine, juice, and champagne. ③ Grapes are the main product that is cultivated in our region. ④ For people who like to know about wine and champagne there are several places where they can learn about the origin of the wine industry, see some of the local products, and taste some of the special wines and champagnes. ⑤ My hometown is a small, quiet city, and its economy is based on agriculture and tourism. ⑥ Additionally, tourism also makes its contribution to the regional economy.

Order of sentences to improve coherence (write the sentence numbers):

Exercise 2.14: Paragraph Coherence

This paragraph lacks coherence. Rewrite the paragraph so that it is more coherent. Use transitions, repeated key words, synonyms, and reference words to improve coherence. Answers may vary. Write your revised paragraph in the space provided.

My own experiences and my observations of others support the generalization that one must seek a deeper reason for the anger within oneself rather than looking to the outside. It is true that anger can be generated from relationships with others, but it is we ourselves who feel it. When we are frustrated by something, the degrees of anger vary according to our character, situation, place, and, scientifically, our genetic orientation. We have the experience of reacting differently to the same situation depending on our mood. We cannot rely on the external factors to change so that we can avoid anger because anger is an internal reaction to what is happening around us. Anger and the situations that cause anger are unavoidable, but we can train ourselves to deal with anger so that anger does not overcome us and affect other people in negative ways.

Exercise 2.15: Using Transitions for Coherence in a Paragraph

Choose an appropriate transition word or phrase to fill each blank in the paragraph. Think about the logical connection that needs to be made between the ideas. Answers may vary.

The Internet affects our lives in many ways today. ① _____, we can

communicate with each other by email easily, compared to sending messages by postal

mail. ② _____, we can chat with our friends, no matter where they are.

③ _____, we can buy whatever we want on the Internet, and we do not

need to go out to the shops. ④ _____, we can pay our bills such as electric

fee and gas fee, and manage our accounts online. ⑤ _____, the Internet

has some disadvantages for people. There is too much information on the Internet that is

not very useful for us, and some information from the Internet is not accurate at all.

⑥ _____, the Internet reduces the interaction of people to some extent.

⑦ _____, your friend may just send an email to you instead of visiting you

in person. That will decrease the opportunities for you to meet each other face to face.

⑧ _____, people can just chat at home on the Internet rather than going

out with their friends. ⑨ _____, while the Internet may make our lives more

convenient in many ways, the Internet also decreases our social interaction and makes our

lives more isolated.

Exercise 2.16: Using Transitions for Coherence in an Essay

The transitions have been deleted in this essay on pages 29–30. Provide an appropriate transition for each blank space to create coherence. Answers may vary.

Employment and Taxes

① _____, many developing countries face economic problems resulting from different factors. Some people claim that the problems are too difficult to solve. There are, ② _____, positive ways to improve the economic situation of countries and promote the lives of their poor people. These must include an increase in job opportunities and a decrease in the amount of taxes. Increasing employment and decreasing taxes will improve the economic situation of a country and reduce the rate of poverty.

③ _____ , employment is the active engine that keeps a country going. It is the means by which people are able to care for themselves and their families. ④ _____, job opportunities maintain a certain economic security for people and enable them to improve their lives. This means that they can care for their families and be active, contributing citizens. ⑤ _____ , jobs are a symbol of independence and self-sufficiency. A person who is self-sufficient does not need the help of governmental social programs like welfare or medical insurance for assistance in his or her life. ⑥ _____, this individual's self-sufficiency would save money for the government.

⑦ _____, unemployment is the negative condition that keeps an economy in an unfavorable and inactive state. Lack of employment is a serious problem for the individual in the sense that he or she will be and will feel dependent and lost. ⑧ _____, he or she may depend on the government to provide the basic needs for him or her. The government, ⑨ _____, loses resources and money in supporting such a person.

⑩ _____, another economic aspect that negatively affects a government is high taxes. Most people complain too much about the large amount of taxes they have to pay to the government. They claim that they cannot afford necessities because they find themselves left with little money. They cannot save money for later situations of need because the amount of their taxes is far out of proportion to their income. Taxes which are too great and which put a person in a tight situation badly affect the population and the economy. ⑪ _____, some economists assert that there should be low, fair, and balanced tax regulations that take into consideration people's personal financial situations and create opportunities for them to live a better life. ⑫ _____, despite economists' strong support of low taxes, it must be emphasized that they do not want taxes to be eliminated altogether. They realize governments must have revenues to use in social services and job creation. Before setting tax levels, governments should provide jobs to enhance people's economic situation. ⑬ _____, there should be a fair decision about the amount of taxes to be paid, taking into account the cost of living and the person's ability to pay a certain amount.

⑭ _____ , high rates of unemployment and high taxes cause economic problems and lead governments into many financial crises. It is only by giving serious consideration to people's financial situations and providing them with jobs that an economy can be improved and stimulated.

PATTERNS OF ORGANIZATION

Narrative Essay

Process Essay

Comparison/Contrast Essay

Cause-and-Effect Essay

Argument Essay

Narrative Essay
[*Handbook*, Section 3A, pages 62–67]

Exercise 3.1: Ordering a Narrative Paragraph

Put the sentences in narrative order by numbering them 1–14. The first one has been done for you as an example.

_____ a. Meanwhile, the campers were talking about how much fun the night was going to be.

_____ b. I don't know what the others wished for, but I wished that I would again have as much fun at the next year's camp.

_____ c. This was upsetting because we all wanted to have a last chance to all be together and have fun.

_____ d. That was when we found out that it was one of the best nights for seeing meteor showers.

__1__ e. One of my best memories took place when I was working at a children's summer camp last year.

_____ f. On Thursday, the counselors and campers had planned a big bonfire and then, later, a star-gazing session, but it had rained heavily.

_____ g. After dinner, we all gathered in a big clearing by the lake and lit the bonfire we had prepared.

_____ h. It was the last weekend for many of the children at camp and everyone was feeling a bit sad.

_____ i. For hours, we all watched shooting stars together.

_____ j. All day, the counselors searched for dry wood and set it up for the bonfire.

_____ k. As the bonfire died down, we all brought out our blankets and lay down to look at the stars.

_____ l. So the next night, everyone was even more eager to have end-of-the-summer fun.

_____ m. We sang songs and roasted marshmallows.

Exercise 3.2: Practice with *When* and *While*

Connect the sentences using *when, while,* or *whenever.* If more than one can be used, write both answers on the line provided.

1. _____ he was a junior in college, he met his future wife.

2. We were just leaving the baseball field _____ a tornado struck.

3. _____ I was watching TV, my brother came home from football practice.

4. _____ they learned that their daughter had been in an accident, they immediately rushed to the hospital.

5. _____ I was young, I used to spend a lot of time at my grandparents. I have fond memories of Sunday mornings spent reading the comics section with my grandfather _____ my grandmother washed the breakfast dishes. To this day, _____ I hear the noise of dishes being washed, I think of those happy times.

6. I had asked my neighbor many times not to play loud music in the afternoon _____ my baby was sleeping, but he would not stop. _____ I just couldn't take it anymore, I finally had to complain to the building manager.

7. At camp, since I didn't like to swim, I would help prepare lunch _____ the other campers were enjoying swimming in the lake.

8. Do you remember a day _____ you were so happy you wished that day could last forever?

Process Essay
[*Handbook*, Section 3B, pages 67–72]

Exercise 3.3: Practice with Process Words and Phrases

Underline the process words or phrases in the paragraph. The first one has been done for you as an example.

How to Find a Doctor

Choosing a physician who will oversee your health care can be a difficult decision, but the process can be made less stressful by following a few simple steps. It is important to work through this process before you urgently need health care, so that you can make a wise and carefully thought-out decision. An initial step in this process is to ask friends for recommendations. Although your experience with a particular doctor may differ from another person's, these opinions can be very valuable in helping you to narrow your search to just a few doctors. Once you have a list of several doctors for whom you have received personal recommendations, you should call each office to ask a few questions: Is the practice accepting new patients? Can the doctor address your (or your family's) particular health concerns? You should also note whether the staff seem professional and friendly. Another very important step in this process is to find out whether your insurance company will cover visits to the physician that you select. You should check with both your insurance company and the doctor's office to verify this. If the answers to your initial questions are positive, a subsequent but optional step is to visit the office in person. Besides determining the convenience of the location, you can observe the atmosphere of the waiting room and examination rooms, and the personalities and mannerisms of the office staff and nurses. A visit also gives you the opportunity to interview the physician and ascertain his or her personality and approach to health care. To complete the process of selecting a doctor, you should inform both the doctor's office and your insurance company of your decision, so that there are no delays or complications when the time comes for you and your family to rely on your doctor's expertise.

Exercise 3.4: Connecting Ideas Using Process Words and Phrases

Connect and/or change the sentences to create a process paragraph. Not every sentence will need to be changed. Some sentences may need to be combined. Answers will vary. Write your paragraph in the space provided.

How to Choose a Major

In choosing a major you should . . .

1. Talk with an advisor at your college or university.

2. Ask your friends if they know any good advisors at your college or university. Try to choose an advisor with interests similar to yours so you can be sure that he or she will have valuable information to share.

3. Tell the advisor about yourself.

4. Let the advisor know what you think your interests are.

5. He or she will give you advice about which departments might be the best for you.

6. Go to the department(s) that your advisor recommended and get more information.

7. Be sure to carefully consider the information you have collected.

8. Discuss the information and your options with friends and family.

9. Consider their advice and your own inclination.

10. Make an informed decision.

Comparison/Contrast Essay
[*Handbook,* Section 3C, pages 73–81]

Exercise 3.5: Connecting Ideas Using Comparison/Contrast Words and Phrases

Connect the pairs of phrases using comparison/contrast vocabulary. Try not to use the same connecting word(s) more than once. Write one comparison and one contrast sentence. Answers will vary.

<u>Example</u>

big cities / small towns

    a. **Both** *big cities* **and** *small towns must offer public education for their children.* [comparison]

    b. **However,** *in big cities, schools are usually overcrowded,* **while** *in small towns, classes are small.* [contrast]

1. *Internet shopping / shopping in a store*

    a.

    b.

2. *older people / younger people*

    a.

    b.

3. *fast food restaurant / sit-down restaurant*

    a.

    b.

4. *eating with a fork / eating with chopsticks*

    a.

    b.

5. *tropical climate / temperate climate*

    a.

    b.

3: Patterns of Organization   37

Exercise 3.6: Using Comparison/Contrast Words to Create a Paragraph

Using comparison/contrast vocabulary, create an effective paragraph based on the framework of information given. Use the chart to take notes. Add any additional points. Answers will vary. Write your paragraph in the space provided.

A. *Cell Phone Plans in the U.S.*	**B.** *Cell Phone Plans in Another Country*
Cost of phone:	Cost of phone:
Available accessories:	Available accessories:
Price per minute:	Price per minute:
Prices at different times of the day and night/weekend:	Prices at different times of the day and night/weekend:
Different plans:	Different plans:
Ability to call internationally:	Ability to call internationally:
Additional points:	Additional points:

Cause-and-Effect Essay
[*Handbook,* Section 3D, pages 82–86]

Exercise 3.7: Identifying Cause-and-Effect Words and Phrases

Underline the cause-and-effect words and phrases.

The Changing of the World with the Advent of the Internet

Imagine a situation where the current Internet system does not work any more. You can see long lines of people who are waiting to pay bills at banks. At the beginning of the semester, college offices are filled with students who want to register for their classes. Unemployment is up as many people working at companies based on the Internet are out of work. Clearly, even though less than twenty years have passed since the Internet started to become commonly used, we can realize that the Internet has greatly affected many parts of our lives.

First of all, the most important effect of the Internet has been to increase accessibility of information. The Internet allows people to get information easily, no matter the place or time. People do not need to go to the library and read several books to get information. That is because Google, the most popular web search engine, can show the web pages containing information people are searching within just a few seconds. Likewise, conventional encyclopedias in the library are not used so much any more because most people use Wikipidia, one of the biggest information providers on the Internet. Thus, most students, researchers, and even common people would be very inconvenienced if the Internet were no longer available. This demonstrates the important position the Internet holds in our daily lives.

Moreover, the Internet has played a great role in facilitating interpersonal communication. For supporting examples one need look no further than email. Today, most students and workers turn on their computer in the morning and check email first. To send and receive email takes less than one minute. Many international students also use Skype, the Internet messenger program, to talk with their family. This program does not involve high cost or much time compared to phone calls or letters. As a consequence, people feel free to contact even those who are very far away using the Internet. This definitely has a positive impact on foreign students, who are far from home and may be feeling lonely due to culture shock. The fact that these students can easily communicate with their friends and family abroad leads to a sense of community and well-being that may help them through their period of culture shock.

Moreover, online shopping has become quite popular as a result of the now common use of the Internet. In my observation, most people know the first step to buy products at a cheaper price is to search at sites such as Amazon. In fact, today, there are lots of online shopping malls that sell products at reasonable prices compared to regular malls because online shopping mall owners do not need to pay for rent. Also, customers do not need to drive to the mall, so they can save time as well as money. This is another way in which the Internet has greatly affected our lives.

Finally, the most striking effect of the Internet has been the advent of online services. Today, people use many kinds of online services. People often pay bills using online banking. Students tend to register for classes or hand in their homework online. Many governments provide online services including registration for the driver's test and photo ID to shorten citizens' waiting time at the office. Because it is so simple, using online services has become part of our daily lives as well, and the Internet is the phenomenon that has made it possible.

The Internet has greatly affected our lives. It helps us access information easily any place or time. We can communicate with those who live very far away using email and some Internet-based programs at less cost and in less time. Furthermore, not only online shopping but also online services make it possible to decrease our effort to go to the store, bank, and government offices. Our lives have gradually changed due to the Internet so that now we might even say it has become a necessity.

Exercise 3.8: Connecting Ideas Using Cause-and-Effect Words and Phrases

Use words or phrases to connect cause-and-effect ideas in the paragraph by filling the blanks. The first one has been done for you as an example. Answers may vary. [Sentences are numbered only for reference in this exercise.]

In the U.S. the divorce rate continues to rise every year. ① *One reason for* this constant increase is the fact that divorces have become so common. Before the 1980s, divorced people were not looked on as the norm. The commonly accepted belief was that these people should have tried harder to work out their marital difficulties. Now, however, ② _____ such a high percentage of married people get divorced, it may seem like a normal part of life. With more than 50% of marriages in the U.S. eventually ending in divorce, no one can take the attitude that divorced people are "strange." In addition, ③ _____ there is no longer a social taboo against getting a divorce, people do not feel compelled to "stick it out." ④ _____ a situation in which couples may go into a marriage thinking, "If it doesn't work out, I can always get a divorce." A typical ⑤ _____ of this kind of thinking is that when a difficult problem arises, rather than working hard to solve it or accepting that a compromise might be the only way to solve the problem, the couple uses divorce as a solution.

Argument Essay
[*Handbook,* Section 3E, pages 87–95]

Exercise 3.9: Identifying Argument Words and Phrases

Underline the argument words and phrases used in the text. Remember that cause-and-effect expressions can also contribute to the development of an argument.

Early Computer Education:
Its Negative Effects on the Intellectual Development of Children

Imagine a group of kindergartners sitting in front of their computers in the computer room of an elementary school. They look into the dazzling images on their individually assigned computer screen while hardly talking to each other. No smile or liveliness can be found in this room, where these 6-year-old children start learning how to adapt themselves to the so-called age of information technology. Even though the computer is now an essential part of modern life, it doesn't seem logical to waste valuable childhood years when children should be performing creative activity and discovering life for themselves. In fact, this type of computer education in early elementary years has several negative effects on the intellectual development of children: lowering their concentration on a task, preventing them from acquiring social skills, and exposing them to a hazardous online environment.

First of all, early computer education can lower children's concentration on a task. While young children learn on the computer, they use lots of software or computer games which contain dazzling pictures. Even though they seem to pay attention to the work on the computer, actually they are just looking at the monitor, overwhelmed by the glittering images. This strong visual stimulation irritates children's minds and the children are apt to lose interest in things without such a brilliant screen. It seems for them so boring and dumb to read a storybook because it is not moving fast or dazzling. As a result, children can be easily distracted and cannot concentrate on the important tasks for their ages such as reading books, writing their opinions, or solving logical problems, which are definitely needed for their academic success and mental growth. We can deduce that this will lead to problems for the children later in life when these skills are necessary.

Another negative effect of early computer education is that children lose time and opportunity to socialize with peers. Because most children tend to work on the computer alone for a long time, they confine themselves in virtual space and are reluctant to interact with peers. Even though they need lots of social experiences in early childhood to grow into a well-rounded person, children can be easily involved in computer activity and may spend all of their free time doing something on the computer. Consequently, they are deprived of important opportunities to play and talk with their friends. It is reasonable to assume, then, that in this type of situation, where children grow up into adults without sufficient opportunity to interact with peers, they may have less of a capability to participate in our complex and interactive society.

Finally, children can be exposed to the hazardous online environment. For example, there is a great deal of inappropriate material on the Internet like pornography, violence, and hatred. Those things exert a very bad influence on children. Because children are so sensitive and do not have much knowledge of life, they accept the dangerous influences as reality. In addition, they can encounter bullies or molesters via chatting or email. Due to the anonymity, a criminal can easily approach the innocent children and lure them into a very harmful situation. Therefore, children may experience physical danger as well.

In conclusion, early computer education may have a negative impact on children with respect to the development of concentration and social skills and to the possibility of harmful Internet experiences. Therefore, it is better to teach children how to use a computer in their later elementary grades, taking into consideration their developmental stages. In doing this, we will be able to minimize the negative effects of children's computer education.

Exercise 3.10: Connecting Ideas Using Logical Argument

Insert one or two sentences that logically connect Statements A and C in each of the groups of argument sentences.

Example

    A. Most college students have many things to do in addition to their school-work.

    B. For example, many students have part-time jobs and participate in extra-curricular activities such as sports and clubs. These activities may be time-consuming and can detract from the time students spend on studying.

    C. Consequently, having tests helps students stay focused on their schoolwork.

Argument 1

    A. The amount of violence on television seems to be steadily increasing.

    B.

    C. Parents must therefore pay close attention to what their children watch on television.

Argument 2

    A. Antioxidants such as beta-carotene and lycopene are found in many fruits and vegetables.

    B.

    C. Thus, diets rich in fruits and vegetables may help reduce the risk of cancer.

Exercise 3.11: Making Generalizations

Write a generalization that can be made for each group of sentences. Answers may vary.

1. Heesung, Maria, and Abdullah are all students in an engineering class. Heesung has recently won an award for her research. Maria has a scholarship to study at the university for two years. Abdullah has been elected president of the Student Engineering Organization.

   The students in the engineering class _____

   _____

2. Akiko Yokohama has studied French for nine years. Her brother, Taro, works as a translator for a financial company in Germany. Their mother teaches English at a school in Tokyo.

   Members of the Yokohama family _____

   _____

3. In Hunter's Woods, 25 murders took place last year. There were also 53 cases of robbery and 10 drive-by shootings.

   The city of Hunter's Woods _____

   _____

4. Colleges are using online systems for grading. They are also using online systems for posting syllabi and providing online bulletin boards for students to post on.

   Colleges _____

   _____

5. Parents use lullabies to help put their babies to sleep. Many hospitals use music therapy to help their patients feel better. Many people, after coming home from a long day at work, put some music on to help them relax.

   Music _____

   _____

SECTION 4
RESEARCH PAPER

Summarizing, Paraphrasing, and Using Quotations

Outlining

Thesis Statements: Argument or Report

APA Style References

MLA Style Works Cited

4

Summarizing, Paraphrasing, and Using Quotations [*Handbook*, Section 4D, pages 109–15]

Exercise 4.1: Summarizing

Two passages from student research papers appear on pages 46–47. Write a paraphrased summary of each passage in two or three sentences in the space provided. (A paraphrased summary is a summary using your own words or phrases, your own sentence structure, and your own order of information.) Summaries will vary in how they are expressed but should have similar main ideas.

Passage A: *Bilateral Aid*

Bilateral aid is the direct transfer of specific resources or money between two countries, and many industrialized nations have their own official development agencies. It is rarely a simple grant of money. It is usually a low-interest loan. In many cases, however, it is a tied loan, which means that the recipient country is required to purchase goods and services from the donor country. For example, a country may decide to give a tied loan for the construction of a steel mill. Under the terms of agreement the receiving government will have to buy the needed material and technical assistance from the donor country.

For the last fifty years, bilateral aid has become an important part of industrialized countries' help to third world countries. However, it has been criticized by people who say it cannot significantly promote third world development and does not relieve poverty or support world peace. Some people add that some developing countries have progressed rapidly without any aid. Although bilateral aid is meant to help poor countries, it is clear that there are many problems with it. Bilateral aid is often driven by political concerns, tied to the purchase of products from the donor country, sent to countries without consultation with local communities, given mostly for big projects, and biased toward the donor countries' interests.

_____

_____

_____

Passage B: *Human Security and International Development*

Traditional development economists have worked on how to raise the Gross Domestic Product (GDP) rate in a developing country but have not paid attention to how far people are capable of making choices in their individual lives. Dr. Amartya Sen, an Indian economist at Harvard University, presented the theory of capability, which explains development not only from the perspective of a country's GDP but also in terms of the improvement of the economic capability of individuals, defined as welfare economics (Sen, 1999).

What makes Sen unique is that his work is based on economics and ethical philosophy, which has led him to the view that being developed as a country does not necessarily mean being rich (Sen, 1999). He suggested a new idea in security that is now known as "human security." This is the idea of considering an individual as needing to be protected by international organizations. It is a unique concept and different from the traditional notion of security.

Traditional security implies security of a nation state both economically and militarily. However, nowadays there are people who cannot be protected by the state because of the increasing risk of regional conflict, which may cause internally displaced people, and because of increasing trade activity by multinational companies that are beyond national regulation.

Sen's contribution to the development economy made him the first Asian economist to win a Nobel Prize in economics, and the concept of human security is now commonly known as a major index of development among people working in many development fields.

[Reference: Sen, A. (1999). *Development as freedom*. Oxford, U.K.: Oxford University Press.]

_____

_____

_____

Exercise 4.2: Recognizing Plagiarism

Each original sentence is shown together with the way it was used in a research paper. Decide whether or not the use is plagiarism. Explain your decision by writing the letter of the appropriate reason: A, B, C, D, or E.

Reasons:

A. Not plagiarism: Original words quoted with quotation marks and with citation

B. Not plagiarism: Complete paraphrase with citation

C. Plagiarism: Original words quoted but with no quotation marks

D. Plagiarism: Some paraphrase but sentence structure is the same and some original words are quoted with no quotation marks

E. Plagiarism: Quotation or paraphrase is correct but the citation is missing

<u>Source of Numbers 1–3</u>: Mann, C. C. (2008). Our good earth: Can we save it? *National Geographic, 214,* 80–106. [page 84]

1. *Original sentence:* Researchers and ordinary farmers around the world are finding that even devastated soils can be restored.

   Use: Researchers and ordinary farmers everywhere are finding that even ruined soils can be restored (Mann, 2008, p. 84).

   _____

2. *Original sentence:* The payoff is the chance not only to fight hunger but also to attack problems like water scarcity and even global warming.

   Use: "The payoff is the chance not only to fight hunger but also to attack problems like water scarcity and even global warming" (Mann, 2008, p. 84).

   _____

3. *Original sentence:* Indeed, some researchers believe that global warming can be slowed significantly by using vast stores of carbon to reengineer the world's bad soils.

   Use: Poor soil everywhere can be improved through the use of carbon, which is plentiful, thus controlling global warming to a large extent (Mann, 2008, p. 84).

   _____

Source of Numbers 4–6: Krebs, C. (2006). Using a dialogue journal to build responsibility and self-reliance: A case study. *RE:view, 37,* 173–176. [page 176]

4. *Original sentence:* Journaling in a variety of formats is a skill that can help all students become more proactive throughout their lives.

    Use: All learners can develop the lifelong ability to anticipate and act on situations through journaling, which can be of different types.

    _____

5. *Original sentence:* A dialogue journal can be used in a small group setting, by students of any age, with or without a disability; it can be general or geared to an area of need.

    Use: Krebs asserts, "A dialogue journal can be used in a small group setting, by students of any age, with or without a disability; it can be general or geared to an area of need" (2006, p. 176).

    _____

6. *Original sentence:* It allows students to communicate reflectively and build important life skills while considering choices, initiating new ideas, and resolving problems.

    Use: Valuable skills for living, such as problem solving and weighing alternatives, can be developed through dialogue journal interactions because they allow students to express ideas in a thoughtful way (Krebs, 2006, p. 176).

    _____

7. *Original sentence:* The sociological imagination allows us to go beyond personal experiences and observations to understand broader public issues.

   Use: "The sociological imagination allows us to go beyond personal experiences and observations to understand broader public issues" (Schaefer, 2003, p. 6).

   _____

8. *Original sentence:* It allows us to look beyond a limited understanding of things to see the world and its people in a new way and through a broader lens than we might otherwise use.

   Use: It enables us to think past a simple analysis of things to consider people and the world from a new perspective and through a broader lens than we might otherwise use (Schaefer, 2003, p. 6).

   _____

9. *Original sentence:* Unemployment is unquestionably a hardship for a man or woman without a job.

   Use: Unemployment is unquestionably a hardship for a man or woman without a job (Schaefer, 2003, p. 6).

   _____

10. *Original sentence:* When unemployment is a social problem shared by millions of people, it is appropriate to question the way that a society is structured or organized.

   Use: In his introduction to sociology published in 2003, Schaefer declares that challenging societal organization is reasonable if millions are unemployed (p. 6).

   _____

Outlining
[*Handbook*, Section 4E, pages 116–17]

Exercise 4.3: Ordering Outline Headings

The headings and subheadings of the outline are listed in a jumbled order and with no indentation. Rearrange the list into an outline on the right side of the page. Use numbers, letters, and suitable indentation to indicate sections and to show the relative importance of ideas. Answers may vary.

Essay title:

Adjusting to a New Culture

Headings and subheadings in mixed order:

The balanced phase

Variations in phases

The phase of novelty and excitement

Achieving real understanding

Three phases

The process of adjusting

Finding fault with the food

Looking more deeply at things

Overlap of phases

The drive from the airport

Noticing the good, the bad, and the in-between

Recommendations for adjusting to a new culture

Arrival in the new country

Excitement about the scenery

The phase of negativity

Being met by someone on arrival

Noticing bad behavior patterns

Seeing all people as very interesting

Thesis Statements
[*Handbook*, Section 4F, pages 118–20]

Exercise 4.4: Thesis Statements: Argument or Report

Examine each sentence. If the sentence is the main focus of a report paper, circle R. If it is the main focus of an argument paper, circle A. Also, if the sentence presents an argument, underline the key words that indicate it is argumentative.

1. Many language experts have tried to develop artificial languages that will serve as a vehicle for communication for the whole planet, but none of the systems has achieved its goal.   R   A

2. It can be argued the relationship between the state and its citizens in a country, not the existence of democratic institutions and a high level of national revenues, is what creates conditions to assure the eradication of poverty.   R   A

3. Even though it has given enjoyment to people around the world, Hollywood has done more societal harm than good in most countries.   R   A

4. E-Commerce will play the most important role in the world business market in the near future.   R   A

5. Over the last four years, Trulife Health Plan has increased the number of insurers, reduced health care costs, and managed to operate several roups of providers.   R   A

6. Hot pepper (Capsicum) can be used for flavoring in cooking, and it can also serve as a remedy for some ailments.   R   A

7. In order to be effective and practical, future scheduling techniques must balance two factors: model accuracy and computational complexity.   R   A

8. Even though many experts still reject any application of the intelligent agents based on a Bayesian network in their field, this paper supports that type of application by presenting a practical implementation of this statistical technique in a non-trivial environment.   R   A

9. Wireless computer technology has already had a significant effect in the daily networking communications of many large companies.   R   A

10. Although many people think both countries have the same response to business investment, it can be shown that this is merely a superficial similarity and their responses are in fact completely different due to cultural factors.   R   A

APA Style
[*Handbook*, Section 4J, pages 127–45]

Exercise 4.5: APA References

Use the information provided for each publication to write a References entry in APA format. Use the examples as models.

1. Book with one author

<u>Example</u>

>Wilkins, N. (2008). *Health education in primary schools.* Springfield, MA: Wynton
>   Publications.

>Date of publication: 2002
>Title: Computation, Causation, and Discovery Procedures
>Publisher: CMP Publications
>Place of publication: Menlo Park, CA
>Author: Lisa Glymour

_____

_____

2. Journal article

<u>Example</u>

>Holtgraves, T. (2007). Second language learners and speech act comprehension.
>   *Language Learning, 57,* 595–610.

>Name of Journal: Annals of Internal Medicine
>Date of publication: 2006
>Title: Diagnostics from Sparse Data: Cyber Assistance
>Author: Samuel Horman, Raul Napolitan, and Paul Heckman
>Page numbers: 504–524
>Volume number: 130

_____

_____

3. Article on the Internet by a group (corporate) author

    Example

    American Heart Association. (2007). *Cigarette smoking and cardiovascular disease.*
    Retrieved November 29, 2007, from http://www.americanheart.org/
    presenter.jhtml?identifier=4545

    Author: Multinational Engineering Consortium
    URL: http://www.nmec-i.com/~goappl/antenn2508.htm
    Date of publication: 2006
    Title: Mobile Antenna Systems
    Date of retrieval: January fifth, 2008

    _____

    _____

4. Article in a newspaper on the Internet, author named

    Example

    Kenwood, P. (2008, January 22). What are supermarkets' price cuts really worth?
    Daily Business Review. Retrieved from http://www.dailybusiness.co.uk/news/
    business/analysis-and-features.934138.html

    Title: Suzuki Case Continues Despite Insurance Settlements
    URL: http://www.newspapers.com/main/nt?s=Jtimes&gwp=p13
    Date of publication: Twenty-seventh February, 2004
    Author: Seymour Berry
    Name of newspaper: Japan Times

    _____

    _____

5. Journal article on the Internet, with DOI assigned

Example

> Wilson. P. T., Braithwaite, C., Wong, S. L., & Lewis, M. (2001). Treating plantar fasciitis. *International Journal of Muscular Therapeutics, 27(3)*, 143–149. doi: 81.2387/d0002-c6754.27.3.143

Page numbers: 41–48

DOI: 96.45978:r0104-p9572.45.4.99

Date of publication: 2000

Author: Simon H. Maripan and Leon DaSilva

Volume number: 115

Name of Journal: Library Journal

Issue number: 3

Title: Democracy and public library patrons

_____

_____

6. Non-print publication (may not be on the Internet)

Example

> Besson, L. (Director). (2001). The big blue [Motion picture]. France: Sony Pictures.

Place of publication: Ecuador

Author: Kenneth Kramer (Photographer)

Date of publication: 2008

Name of publisher: Galleria Montalban

Title: Galapagos Images: Reptile Haven [Photographs]

_____

_____

MLA Style
[*Handbook*, Section 4K, pages 146–62]

Exercise 4.6: MLA Works Cited

Use the information provided for each publication to write a Works Cited entry in MLA format. Use the examples as models.

1. Book with one author

Example

    Pinker, Steven. *How the Mind Works.* New York: W.W. Norton Company, 1997.
        Print.

    Medium of publication: Print
    Date of publication: 2008
    Author: David Collinson
    Publisher: SportPros Press
    Place of publication: San Francisco
    Title: The Science of Pole Vaulting

_____

_____

2. Journal article

Example

    Douglas, Harris and Carolyn Herrington. "Accountability, Standards, and the
        Growing Achievement Gap: Lessons from the Past Half Century." *American*
        Journal of Education 112.2 (2006): 209–38. Print.

    Volume number: 32
    Title: Sculpture in Transition: The Work of Gian Lorenzo Bernini
    Name of Journal: Classical Art Studies
    Date of publication: 1990
    Medium of publication: Print
    Authors: Lewis Continelli, Helmut Logan, and Lianne Marshall
    Issue number: 1
    Page numbers: 183–95

_____

_____

3. Article on the Internet by a group (corporate) author

Example

Environmental Services Association. *Controlling Carbon Monoxide in the Workplace.* 1997. Web. 20 Oct. 2008.

Date of publication: 2007

Title: How Architecture Influences Life

Date of retrieval: December fourteenth, 2007

Medium of publication: Web

Author: Portland Association of Architects

_____

_____

4. Article in a newspaper on the Internet, author named

Example

Southwood, Paul. "No Respite for Hospital Workers." *Denver Gazette.* Midwest Publications Consortium, 22 Nov. 2007. Web. 3 Jan. 2008.

Medium of publication: Web

Name of publisher/owner of website: Ontario Media

Author: Anne Kingsley

Date of retrieval: September twenty-fifth, 2007

Title: Building a Green Town Center.

Name of newspaper: Toronto Times

Date of publication: August fourteenth, 2004

_____

_____

5. Journal article on the Internet

Example

Stewart, William, and David Mackenzie. "A Macroeconomic Analysis of Two State Fiscal Policies." *Online Journal of Economics* 18.3 (2005): 72–81. Web. 13 Apr. 2006.

URL: http://www.edusocial.edu/ir/library/pdf/pp4.0340.pdf
Title: Life in the Steel Mills: Workers in the Front Line
Date of publication: 1983
Name of Journal: Teaching Social Studies
Date of retrieval: August twentieth, 2005
Page numbers: 221–32
Issue number: 1
Authors: Jonas Kasevitch and Stewart McTavish
Medium of publication: Web
Volume number: 45

_____

_____

6. Non-print publication (may not be on the Internet)

[As medium of publication, note the digital file type or other medium, for example, GIF file, JPEG file, TIFF file, PDF file, *Microsoft Word* file, DVD.]

Example

Cortez, Emilio. "Dance Moves: Salsa for You!" 2004. Studio Uno de Argentina. JPEG file.

Date of publication: 2008
Authors: Jeremy Kerr and Fred Wilson
Name of publisher: Community College Media
Digital file type or other medium of publication: GIF file
Title: Animation Techniques in Vocational Training

_____

_____

SECTION 5
GRAMMAR AND STYLE

At Word Level

Word Form

Articles

Prepositions

Word Choice in Formal Writing Style

Reference Words

Reducing Wordiness

At Sentence Level

Subject-Verb Agreement

Run-On Sentences and Sentence Fragments

Comma Splice

Relative Clauses: Restrictive and Non-Restrictive

Parallel Structure

Sentence Combining

Sentence Variety

5

Word Form
[*Handbook*, Section 5A, pages 164–65]

Exercise 5.1: Word Form

Correct the word form error(s) in the sentences.

1. The lens acted as a prism, making the light looked like a rainbow.

2. Most of the mouse were used as control in the experiment.

3. The most common used material for computer casing is a type of polymer.

4. War are usually fought because a political power decides it wants more land.

5. The shipping of computer from the factory is usually done on Mondays and Wednesdays.

6. By law, families must use car seats for all child eight years old or younger.

7. After the invited speaker finished to talk, she took questions from the audience.

8. It is important to be diplomat when dealing with a matter involving the development of a peace treaty among nations.

9. At the library you can find many different type of books.

10. Before write the paper, students should to make an outline.

Articles
[*Handbook*, Section 5B, pages 165–69]

Exercise 5.2: Articles

In the paragraph, fill in the blanks with *a/an*, *the*, or 0 for zero article. Answers may vary in some contexts.

My hobby is oil painting. I often used to go to ① _____ museum to look at

② _____various paintings. Among the artists, I preferred ③ _____ canvases of Maurice Utrillo,

④ _____ French painter who mainly drew Montmartre in Paris. Utrillo had three phases in his

painting life: ⑤ _____ "montagny period," ⑥ _____"colorist period," and ⑦ _____"white

period." I prefer ⑧ _____ paintings from the last phase. ⑨ _____ first paintings he did are

only like imitations of ⑩ _____impressionists, and I cannot feel my favorite whitish mood

from his canvases. ⑪ _____ paintings from ⑫ _____ "colorist period" give us ⑬ _____

cheerful but too bright impression. On the other hand, Utrillo's paintings from ⑭ _____

"white period" move me deeply. ⑮ _____ whitish colors with ⑯ _____various tones make

me feel melancholy. In addition, ⑰ _____ various tones of whites give me ⑱ _____

impressions of loneliness and isolation. I enjoy viewing ⑲ _____Utrillo's paintings alone to

feel those moods and emotions that only he gives us through his "white period," and when I

paint ⑳ _____ pictures, I often imitate these tones because I wish to create ㉑ _____ similar

melancholy feeling.

Exercise 5.3: Looking at Nouns in Context to Determine Article Use

Underline the nouns in the paragraph from a student essay. For each noun, notice whether *the*, *a/an*, or *zero article* is used with it. For each noun, give a reason for the type of article or zero article. [The sentences are numbered only for reference in this exercise.] <u>Note:</u> The meaning of a noun may also be limited or made more definite by using demonstratives (e.g., *those*), possessives (e.g., *my*), and quantifiers (e.g., *some*). In such cases, articles are not used.

   ① I remember one day when I was traveling to another city by train. ② The journey was very long. ③ Sitting next to me there was a family who had annoying and unbearable children. ④ It was a long and horrible day for me. ⑤ I had to bear the noise and misbehavior of the children. ⑥ I know that children make noise. ⑦ They go through a noisy phase that is part of life. ⑧ That's their job. ⑨ The children were only being children, doing what children do. ⑩ However, there is a limit to everything. ⑪ Those children went far beyond the limit. ⑫ As a passenger, I am entitled to have a peaceful and quiet environment when traveling. ⑬ These parents should have kept their children quiet. ⑭ Before taking a long trip, parents should teach their children how to behave in a public place or when using public transportation. ⑮ In this way, neither the passengers nor the parents would have a hard time on their trip, and everybody would be relaxed, especially me!

Prepositions
[*Handbook*, Section 5C, pages 170–71]

Exercise 5.4: Prepositions

Insert the correct preposition in each gap in the paragraph. The first two have been done for you as examples.

I did hair cuts ① _for_ some friends recently, and I realized the process of hair-cutting is similar ② _to_ the writing process. When you start to cut hair for somebody, you need to figure ③ _____ the best style for this person, so you consult ④ _____ her or him, give some suggestions, and get some feedback. This is the same as generating ideas ⑤ _____ writing. Then you start cutting the hair ⑥ _____ the shape you designed. ⑦ _____ this stage, you don't work ⑧ _____ the details, but rather cut the hair ⑨ _____ each area such that you get a basic style. This phase compares ⑩ _____ drafting in writing. As you go on, you may find that the hairstyle you designed first is not good enough ⑪ _____ some ways. Therefore, you need to change it to fit the shape ⑫ _____ the person's face. Revising for writing is the same. Although this phase is similar for both hair-cutting and writing, there is a little difference ⑬ _____ them. In writing, you can delete some paragraphs and write new ones, but in hair-cutting you cannot put ⑭ _____ the hair that you have cut ⑮ _____. Last, when you are happy ⑯ _____ the shape and style of the haircut, you need to work ⑰ _____ some details, like the final editing stage in writing. You can smooth the edges ⑱ _____ the hair, or put some gel ⑲ _____ it, while in your essay you may want to check the spelling, punctuation, citations, or bibliography.

Exercise 5.5 Phrasal Verbs

In each sentence a phrasal verb (verb plus one or more prepositions) is underlined. From the list of verbs, select one for each sentence to express a similar idea more formally. Use the correct form of the verb, and change any other grammar as necessary. The first one has been done for you as an example. One word is not used. Write your answers in the space provided.

analyze	cancel	~~confuse~~	continue
discard	discover	finish	fluctuate
improve	reduce	tolerate	

1. In his answer, Maurice <u>mixed up</u> two theories that should have been kept separate.

   In his answer, Maurice confused two theories that should have been kept separate.

2. Katherine can't <u>put up with</u> people who act in a superior manner.

3. We must carefully <u>break</u> this problem <u>down</u> into its components before we can find a solution.

4. When Anna <u>gets through with</u> the first project, she will immediately start the next one.

5. The dietician told me that I must <u>cut down on</u> my salt intake.

6. Octavia must <u>keep on</u> studying hard if she wants to pass the test

7. Professor Benatar <u>found out</u> why the volcano was emitting lava.

8. Leo <u>threw away</u> the damaged equipment.

9. The data indicate that the temperatures <u>go up and down</u> very much.

10. Due to bad weather, we had to <u>call off</u> our field trip to the science center.

Word Choice in Formal Writing Style
[*Handbook*, Section 5D, pages 172–73]

Exercise 5.6: Word Choice

The short essay includes a variety of informal and general words, some of which have been underlined, and there may be additional words that you think are general and/or informal. Replace them with more formal or specific words above the underlined word(s). Be prepared to discuss your answers. Some word changes may require changing the sentence structure or adding a longer noun phrase. Answers may vary. [Paragraphs are numbered only for reference in this exercise.]

Away from Home

1. When I left my country and moved away from my family, I needed to learn new things. For example, I was awful at cooking before I came here, but now I am a good cook. Furthermore, I eat proper food and pay more attention to what I eat because if I get sick, nobody will take care of me. Although I do not have lots of time to spend on eating and cooking, I still insist on eating regularly and at home.

2. Another effect of leaving the family is having to manage everything better and without help. For instance, I have more time than before, and I can decide how to spend it. I do not need to get permission to do anything. I have made a study schedule for myself and have been following it day by day. It has already taken my parents lots of money to let me study here. Thus, I should manage my money well by not buying luxury things, comparing prices, and using coupons when I make purchases.

3. Finally, leaving my family and living by myself has been good for me because it made me grow up fast and get a sense of independence. It is very difficult for me to get used to this kind of life. Some things have changed and are different from before, such as my diet and my time and money management. However, I think I am getting an important and helpful influence for my whole life. Such experiences are good for all people.

Reference Words
[*Handbook*, Section 5E, pages 174–77]

Exercise 5.7: Reference Words

Correct wrong or unclear references in each sentence, or insert synonyms in place of repetitive words or phrases. Answers may vary.

1. Professor Davis told Professor Lawson that his students were hard workers.

2. If the nations of the world all agreed to apply the same policies, they would be more successful.

3. Athletics at the Olympic level requires dedicated daily training. They actually spend years of their lives working towards this goal.

4. Our political campaign was helped by several unexpected global conflicts. The conflicts changed the way that voters were thinking about us.

5. Mary told me that there were two ways to interpret the experiment's results: one was that it was a well-conducted experiment and another was that its design was weak. I had not previously thought it was an issue.

6. The diplomats have refused to negotiate a ceasefire agreement, which is not acceptable.

7. The factory managers told the other employees that they would be getting an increase in their pay.

8. We emailed the office of the daily newspaper about the latest news, but it did not reply.

9. The typical romantic movie, it presents an unreal view of life.

10. Miguel said that I should be able to speak Spanish fluently because I lived there for a long time.

Reducing Wordiness
[*Handbook*, Section 5F, pages 177–79]

Exercise 5.8: Reducing Wordiness in Sentences

Revise the sentences to reduce wordiness. Write your answers in the space provided. Answers may vary.

1. His argument is not very persuasive because it is a weak argument that provides little evidence to show that it is valid.

2. After reading her report, we decided that the hiring policy regarding new workers should not be applied in our consideration of the hiring of anyone new.

3. If economists were to base their recommendations only on the data they receive from corporations, their recommendations would not be based on enough information to give good advice.

4. It is the opinion of Mrs. MacDonald that we should not support any politicians who promise that everything will become perfect in the future if we vote for them.

5. From my viewpoint, study skills are very important skills that we can acquire that will help us when we are studying in school or college to advance our education.

Exercise 5.9: Reducing Wordiness in a Paragraph

Revise the paragraph to reduce wordiness. Write your answer in the space provided. Answers may vary.

These days there are many people exhibiting different types of behavior. Usually people's attitudes in a society and their behavior toward each other and society depend on the education and training they received from their parents when they were young, and that affects their future and their whole lives later on. Based on my own experience and people's habits in a society, it can be shown that parents influence their children's future. During my childhood, my parents taught me good values, the kind of attitudes that should be adopted socially and in every way, according to each situation of my life. In order to give me some proofs and examples, they also used to put into practice these values whenever it was necessary for them, and I grew up with those kinds of attitudes. They taught me honesty, integrity, and courtesy toward all.

Subject-Verb Agreement
[*Handbook*, Section 5H, pages 182–84]

Exercise 5.10: Subject-Verb Agreement

If there is an error in the sentence, write I ("incorrect") in the blank, and correct the error. If there is no error, write C ("correct") in the blank.

_I_   1. Even though the answer ~~are~~ *is* correct, the way in which you got the answer is not clear.

_I_   2. Each of the twelve questions ~~have~~ *has* only one correct answer.

_C_   3. They decided to meet on Thursday to finish writing their programs, which are due on Friday.

_I_   4. In order to solve these ~~problem~~ *problems*, we need to first look at what is causing them.

_I_   5. Neither my teacher nor my advisor ~~know~~ *knows* the answer.

_C_   6. Many of the characters in the novel *The Lord of the Rings* are based on beings from Celtic mythology.

_I_   7. Both of the societies that we are studying in our textbook right now ~~seems~~ *seem* to share a common ideological foundation.

Either   8. It has been proven that the majority of the population in each of those countries *do* / does not vote in the annual election.

_I_   9. It is difficult to determine whether the parent or the child ~~were~~ *was* to blame.

_I_ 10. The news these days ~~are~~ *is* full of stories of violence.

Run-On Sentences and Sentence Fragments
[*Handbook,* Section 5I, pages 184–86]

Exercise 5.11: Fragments

Revise the sentences in the paragraph to correct the two sentence fragment errors.

In King Louis 14th's era, arts and new technologies were the most important ways of advertising. He and his court encouraged many kinds of arts and technology. To represent the power of the king. In the field of art, he established an organization of painters and patronized many artists including famous sculptors and architects. The Académie Française was established at this time. Since he wanted scholars to be studying the French language and to be cultivating it. In the field of science, we can say that the establishment of the national astronomical observatory was one of his main achievements.

Exercise 5.12: Run Ons and Fragments

Correct any run-on or fragment errors. Write your answers in the space provided. Answers may vary.

King Louis 14th demanded that the painters paint him as a god or mythological person and add more dignity to his portrait. The king in the paintings was thus painted wearing clothes of the emperors of ancient Rome and Greece, to send a message that he was the legitimate successor of the ancient empires. In these paintings, there were also goddesses and legendary heroes around the king to impress people with his honorable character. Moreover, the height of the king in paintings was always bigger than his real height, all of the images were made to strengthen the authority of the king and government.

The famous palace of Versailles was designed to represent the authority and the power of the king in the clearest way. In this palace, many bureaucrats and noble families lived around the king, who was the center of the court, the paintings or statues of him, as well as his symbols, were placed everywhere in the palace. People were surrounded by works of art, that were well planned to give a special impression. Therefore, it was difficult for citizens to be indifferent to the existence of the king at this palace.

Comma Splice
[*Handbook,* Section 5J, pages 186–88]

Exercise 5.13: Comma Splices

Correct the comma splice errors in the paragraph. Answers may vary.

Everyone needs smiles! You need a smile, for example, when you feel lonely or blue. When you are happy, it takes no effort to smile because it is already there. However, when you feel down, it is good to smile, how? It is easy. Lift your lips' edges. You do not need a big smile, just a little lift makes your mind lighter and warmer. I have to say that I do not know why this works, however, I have heard about a relationship between the physical and mental systems, they are interactive, when you are happy, a smile appears on your face. When you make a smiling face, you can make yourself feel happy. After I heard about this, I tried it, it worked!

Relative Clauses: Restrictive and Non-Restrictive
[*Handbook*, Section 5K, pages 188–90]

Exercise 5.14: Comma Use in Relative Clauses

Correct the errors in relative clauses in the paragraph.

The liver is the most important organ that is affected by alcohol. The liver which is the largest organ in the body removes or detoxifies poisons, germs, and bacteria from the blood, makes protein, and produces immune agents. Although direct damage from alcohol in the liver cells has not been reported, alcohol and its metabolites injure the liver by blocking its normal metabolism of proteins, fats, and carbohydrates. As a consequence, consuming alcohol on a regular basis causes fatty liver, alcoholic hepatitis, and alcoholic liver cirrhosis which all prevent the normal functioning of the body. For example, blood may accumulate in the leg and in the abdomen. In addition, bleeding that cannot be stopped easily develops when the protein-making function of the liver is destroyed. Gallstones, itching, and jaundice which is the yellowing of the skin and eyes also result because of deteriorating bile metabolism. If the liver is not able to detoxify poisons from the blood, these toxins accumulate in the blood and finally in the brain. People who have these problems are likely to suffer from personality changes, mental symptoms, coma, and even death.

Parallel Structure
[*Handbook,* Section 5L, pages 191–92]

Exercise 5.15: Parallel Structure

Find and correct errors in parallelism in the paragraph. Answers may vary.

Governments frequently divert what science produces into war-related uses. The original reason for scientists inventing things is usually to improve technology and helping people live better. For example, the purpose of inventing the airplane was to shorten travel time, and dynamite was invented for people to remove mountains and they could build houses there more easily. However, governments changed the purpose of those technologies. The airplane has been changed into a military equipment transporter or carrying bombs, and they made dynamite into a killing tool in these bombs. It is true that people spend a lot of money on researching new technology for a better life; however, a lot more money is spent for development of the new technology into new weapons.

Sentence Combining
[*Handbook*, Section 5M, pages 193–95]

Exercise 5.16: Combining Sentences

Combine the pairs or groups of simple sentences on pages 75–76. Try to change the meanings as little as possible. Answers may vary.

1. Memory is a vital quality of human thought. Without memory we would not be able to function in our daily activity.

2. Memory failures do happen frequently. This causes many problems, such as forgetting important information that we studied for an exam.

3. When studying for an exam, you can use different techniques to improve how much you remember the important points. You can highlight the points in your textbook with a marker pen. You can write a summary of the important points on file cards. You can recite the important points out loud to yourself.

4. I make up possible exam questions based on my class notes. It's a study method I learned from my aunt. She was a professor of psychology. This method has always been the most effective one for me.

5. Study your class notes before a test. Put the notes aside. Then say the main points out loud, as if you are telling someone what they are. It will help you remember them.

6. I learned a valuable study method from my friend. My friend William seems to remember his class notes very well. It helped me a lot.

7. William advised me not to leave my studying until just before a test. He said that I should have shorter study sessions of the same material every day. He had found this approach to be much more effective than trying to remember everything in one long study session.

8. Memory is affected by repetition. Highlight the important points in your textbook. Read them again and again over a period of several days.

9. Some students use mnemonics to help them remember facts. A mnemonic is a memory aid. A mnemonic can be a made-up word, a verse, or other verbal or visual device.

10. I found it hard to remember the colors of the rainbow. Then I learned a simple mnemonic that sounds like a person's name. The mnemonic is "Roy G. Biv." It uses the first letter of each color: red, orange, yellow, green, blue, indigo, violet.

Exercise 5.17: Using Specific Structures to Revise Sentences

Rewrite the sentences using the suggested structure. Combine sentences when necessary. Answers may vary.

1. I was very unwilling to take the course in trigonometry. I took the course. **[adverb]**

2. During the 1980s Tim Berners-Lee developed the foundation of what we now call the Web with his work on information retrieval from distributed systems. **[passive]**

3. We missed our flight due to Stanley's failure to arrive on time. **[divided sentence]**

4. Janet had studied hard for the final examination in her Biology class. She was sure that she would do very well on it. **[dependent clause]**

5. Paulina was encouraged by her good results on the final History exam. She thought that she might take a more advanced course in the next semester. **[participial phrase]**

6. Alexander Fleming discovered penicillin when he observed that mold would not grow around a bacteria culture that he had unintentionally left uncovered. **[passive]**

7. Alfonso traveled to Ecuador, where his family was still living. He was happy to go there. **[adverb]**

8. I did not say "basketball." I said Enrico is very skilled at tennis. **[divided sentence]**

9. I wished that I had studied harder for the spelling test. I arrived at school in a state of anxiety. **[participial phrase]**

10. It was not easy to develop a new research program to better understand how the sun transmits radiation. Professor Bigelow and her graduate students were successful in their work and published an article about it. **[dependent clause]**

Sentence Variety
[*Handbook,* Section 5N, pages 196–99]

Exercise 5.18: Creating More Variety in Sentence Structure

Rewrite the paragraph so that there is more variety in the sentence structure. Write your answer in the space provided. Answers may vary.

The use of fossil fuels has increased greatly. Coal, natural gas, and oil are fossil fuels. Fossil fuels are becoming hard to find. Using more ethanol would be better than relying too much on fossil fuels. Ethanol has advantages that are clear. Ethanol's big advantage is that it can be made from many common crops. Sugar cane, corn, and wheat are examples of possible sources of ethanol. Growing more of these crops can help farmers increase their income. However, these crops are also needed as food for humans and livestock. A choice has to be made sometimes between growing crops for food and growing crops for fuel. It's a difficult choice. Reducing the supply of food crops causes an immediate increase in food prices. Many of the world's people are hungry and need these crops as food. However, with cheaper fuel, farmers can grow crops more efficiently. They use fuel-powered equipment for planting and reaping crops. This can increase their production of crops.

SECTION 6
PUNCTUATION

Period

Question Mark

Exclamation Point

Comma

Semicolon

Colon

6

Period
[*Handbook*, Section 6A, pages 202–3]

Exercise 6.1: Period at End of Sentence: Run On

Each sentence has a punctuation error that has resulted in a run-on sentence. Correct the error by inserting a period in the appropriate position. Correct capitalization as necessary.

1. Machines can be helpful if you understand them some people don't like any machines.

2. When the sun is shining, I go swimming when it rains, I go swimming too because I love swimming.

3. Compare the two trees that one is a little bit taller than the other.

4. I would very much like to travel to foreign countries as soon as possible which ones I will go to will not be certain until I determine the costs of air travel.

5. The raw material of statistics is data or numbers the data are the result of counting or measurement that assigns numbers to objects.

6. Biostatistics focuses only on biological and medical science areas there are many biostatistics applications in clinical data.

7. Descriptive statistics is organizing and summarizing data to determine what information the data contain to organize and summarize data, we can use methods such as order array or measuring the central tendency by mean, median, and mode for population or grouped data.

8. Diabetes can be divided into two categories one is Insulin Dependent Diabetes and the other is Non-Insulin Dependent Diabetes.

9. Both types of diabetes are related to excess glucose concentration in the blood each has its own causes, symptoms, and treatments.

10. There are many problems in the field of global education basically they arise from the fact that so many children do not attend primary school, so more advanced education is not possible.

Exercise 6.2: Period at End of Sentence: Correcting Errors

In the paragraph, the wrong punctuation has been inserted where the periods should be. Make the necessary corrections.

She looked out to sea, to her left were some ships? Far beyond the ships, she saw some whales and dolphins, she saw only cliffs and crashing waves to her right, she decided then that she would try to find a ship that would accept her as a passenger for the long journey across the ocean? She was determined to cross the Pacific and begin her search—

Exercise 6.3: Period with Decimals

Use numerals with periods in the correct places to express each amount.

1. three and four hundredths _____

2. sixty-four thousand dollars and no cents _____

3. one and six hundredths _____

4. seven and eighty-six hundredths_____

5. two million dollars and two cents _____

6. fourteen and fourteen hundredths _____

Question Mark
[*Handbook*, Section 6B, page 204]

Exercise 6.4: Question Mark and Period

Some of the sentences in the paragraph are questions, and some are not. Place periods or question marks in the appropriate places. Capitalize as necessary. Remember that a question mark is not placed after indirect (reported) questions.

The detective sat in his office thinking about the strange events at the time of the crime

These were his thoughts: Who was the second witness why had she vanished so quickly

there were many people who wanted to know he knew that Anne wanted to know Sally had

asked questions about it Andrew had also made inquiries James, however, had asked only

two questions he had asked when the crime occurred he had also asked why it had been

committed that was very strange why had James not asked about the second witness Did he

perhaps know where she was it would probably be a good idea to question James about his

movements after the crime

Exclamation Point
[*Handbook*, Section 6C, page 205]

Exercise 6.5: Exclamation Point for Strong Feeling

Decide which of the following sentences or phrases express strong feeling, and place exclamation points after them. In other cases, use a period or question mark.

1. Oh, no

2. Is the weather bad

3. The painting was rather unusual, with a turtle shown in a strange mixture of green, blue, pink, and various shades of red

4. How strange

5. Who is that man carrying the book

6. Stop, thief

7. Are you willing to speak to the ambassador

8. What an amazing opportunity

Exercise 6.6: Exclamation Points, Periods, or Question Marks in a Conversation

Place exclamation points, periods, or question marks in the appropriate places in the dialogue.

Customer: How much is this pair of shoes

Clerk: Ninety-nine dollars

Customer: That's so expensive

Clerk: Not really, considering what they are made of

Customer: What are they made of

Clerk: A special, rare material originally designed for astronauts' boots for use in outer space

Customer: How amazing perhaps I'll buy a pair

Comma
[*Handbook*, Section 6D, pages 206–15]

Exercise 6.7: Comma after Introductory or Transitional Words and Phrases

Place commas, if needed, after the introductory words and phrases in the sentences.

1. It is customary to place a comma after introductory or transitional words and phrases.

2. Remembering all the serious obstacles faced the previous year Janet refused to try again.

3. Having defeated the enemy our military forces were withdrawn as soon as it was safe to do so.

4. As a means of repairing torn cloth nothing could be better than this special machine.

5. Being a lazy student from my earliest schooldays I naturally found it hard to pass examinations.

6. George had learned little and had made few friends by the end of the third term.

7. After speaking to his bank manager the wheat farmer was able to get a loan to enable him to continue farming for another year.

8. At the restaurant Ivan and Olga met many journalists whom they had not seen for fifteen years.

9. The letters that were addressed to me were finally delivered to the right address.

10. Except for the writing class my studies at the Language Institute are very easy.

11. After understanding English comma usage the students will find all the other marks of punctuation relatively easy.

12. Moreover it was absolutely impossible for the ambassador to visit the Prime Minister.

Exercise 6.8: Comma after Introductory Clause

Place commas, if needed, after the introductory clauses in the sentences.

1. When winter comes I will go skiing.

2. He will buy a bag of oranges if he goes to the supermarket.

3. After Leo's cousin arrives in Tasmania they will travel together to the north of the island.

4. Very many students agree that the university offers excellent courses.

5. Unless they can travel to an English-speaking country students must learn the language in their own countries.

6. Students who want to learn English travel to English-speaking countries if they can.

7. Because certain unusual events have occurred the detectives are investigating the case.

8. Many people do not smoke because it would affect their health.

9. This exercise will end at number ten so that the students can have a rest.

10. Since you have worked so hard at this exercise you may now stop for a break.

Exercise 6.9: Comma before Coordinating Conjunctions Linking Independent Clauses

Place commas, if needed, before the coordinating conjunctions in the sentences. When both clauses are very short (about five words or less), the commas can be left out to emphasize a strong connection between the clauses.

1. There has been an increase in the popularity of volleyball and many more spectators are attending the games.

2. Some of the tennis players were doing special exercises to improve their game but others were just relaxing in the clubhouse.

3. The women from that country did not like golf nor did they like cricket.

4. Igor will travel to Uruguay to start a new branch of his business or he will stay in his country for two more years and then go to Uruguay.

5. My chemistry teacher keeps very busy since he also does a lot of research.

6. Eddie was ready to fight them but they did not come near him because they were afraid of him.

7. Jane gave me advice and I succeeded.

8. As it was the only drink available at the small cafeteria we drank many cups of strong coffee.

9. The research teams in the computer industry always try to find out what the competition is working on and they then try to bring out similar or better products.

10. To make a good pizza at home, you should have the right ingredients and prepare them in the right way.

Exercise 6.10: Comma with Lists of Words, Phrases, or Clauses

If the sentences include a list of three or more words, phrases, or clauses, separate the items from each other by placing a comma after each item in the list.

1. Books papers bottles cans pens and pencils were lying scattered on the floor of the room.

2. Jennifer decided to study economic theory business administration personnel management and computer programming.

3. Jennifer's sister could not decide whether to study art French or linguistics.

4. James refused to go to the store because it was raining very hard because he felt tired and because there was enough food in the house.

5. If a politician smiles at you promises you something wonderful claims to have done many good things or criticizes his opponents you can guess that there must be an election soon.

6. Financial advice loans and credit cards were all offered by the new bank.

7. The travel advertisement promised an ideal holiday in South America, with visits to Brazil Paraguay Argentina and Chile.

8. The journalist said that all countries need to diversify their energy sources find more fossil fuels and conserve fuel supplies in order to ensure that energy resources are adequate.

9. The complaints to the mayor mentioned problems with parking facilities traffic flow public transportation unsafe pedestrian crossings and special paths for bicycles.

10. Swimming walking jogging and wrestling are all good forms of exercise for busy students.

Exercise 6.11: Comma with Coordinate Adjectives

Separate coordinate adjectives from each other by placing a comma between them. Do not place a comma between the last adjective and the noun. Do not separate cumulative adjectives. (Adjectives that can be joined by *and* are coordinate; adjectives that cannot be joined by *and* are cumulative and are not separated by commas.)

1. Senator Pulinski is a tough outspoken critic of the President's foreign policy.

2. Matilda bought a beautiful bright blue winter coat.

3. It was a difficult bumpy long twisting road that led to the farmhouse on the side of the mountain.

4. The student said that her history class was always interesting very informative and quite stimulating.

5. Due to a severe system-wide problem with spam and viruses, our company installed a complicated computer protection program on all our machines.

6. Our walk in the woods turned out to be cold wet and tiresome instead of the pleasant relaxing stroll that we had expected.

7. The best exhibit in the art gallery was a ten-foot-wide concrete and metal statue of a horse and rider.

8. The Queen's chefs prepared a delicious mildly-spicy special dish for her fifteen dinner guests.

9. Antonio told us that the people he met were helpful kind and hospitable.

10. The Himalayas, where Mount Everest is located, are a huge awe-inspiring mountain range in Asia.

Exercise 6.12: Comma with Quotations

Place commas before and after the direct quotations (the words actually spoken). Leave out the comma when a quotation begins or ends a sentence and when the quotation ends with a question mark or exclamation point.

1. Yoo-Jin wrote "These two advertisements can be compared in several aspects."

2. "The women's salaries are higher than the average salary of men in that business" asserted Nina.

3. "Mr. Kipling" I asked "When did you write that patriotic poem?"

4. Yuki stated emphatically "My company's products are the best in the world!"

5. "This design will appeal to young, fashionable people. We must use it in our next product" said the artist to the manager.

6. "I prefer" said Hannah, pointing at the book "to stay at home alone to read this. It's so interesting! It's about English grammar."

7. "The style and purpose of this musical composition are fascinating" said Jessie.

8. "Online purchases were more than half of the sales in the first quarter, signifying a major new direction for the company" according to a report released by Frew and Macmillan Corporation.

9. A professor of business studies wrote "In electronic transactions, transparency of price, design, availability, and supplier produces more choices and better pricing."

10. "Industrial development near the city is the key to our progress" announced the mayor.

Exercise 6.13: Comma with Abbreviations

Place commas, as needed, in the sentences.

1. The Institute teaches many things very well e.g. grammar and writing.

2. The important issue in this election is tax credits for individual citizens, i.e. indirectly returning some funds to them.

3. During the test you must remove all bags, books, papers etc. from the desk.

4. Smith et al. wrote the book about prehistoric times that I studied in my anthropology course.

5. Abbreviations should be limited to situations where they help the reader, i.e. when comprehension would be increased by using them.

6. Take some extra food, clothing etc. on this trip because it may take longer than planned.

7. I do not support the program promoted by Mr. Ross et al.

8. There are some very good books that you can use to learn about numbers and data analysis e.g. *Statistics and Number Magic*, which was recently published.

Exercise 6.14: Comma with Contrasting or Interrupting Elements or Those Needing Separation for Clarity

Place a comma, if needed, before and after contrasting or interrupting elements or those needing separation for clarity. Omit the first comma if the interrupting element begins the sentence. Omit the second comma if the interrupting element ends the sentence.

1. These blue flowers by contrast do not eat insects.

2. This computer though excellent is not the type they need.

3. Therefore the square of the hypotenuse is equal to the sum of the squares of the other two sides.

4. Would you like to sing now Ms. Johnson?

5. Our shoes are you know the best available even if they are the most expensive.

6. Students who want to attend college must be very diligent.

7. Sounding quite excited she spoke about her trip to New Zealand.

8. I accepted the suggestion of painting the walls red and orange because the room needed brightening.

9. Will you please be as quiet as possible during the recording?

10. Secondly place the apples in a dish with the other fruit.

11. My uncle's boat which I had often played in was lost in last week's hurricane.

12. Our reading teacher bought a fine car from the second hand car dealer on Forbes Avenue.

13. We arrived in this great city in September of 1977.

14. Angela despite her injured foot won the long jump.

15. This book not the one that is on the table is his.

16. I think that given no serious or unexpected obstacles we will complete our research program before the middle of March.

Semicolon
[*Handbook*, Section 6E, pages 216–17]

Exercise 6.15: Semicolon with Independent Clauses

Use semicolons to separate independent clauses, coordinate clauses, or items in a list. (Note that the semicolons are made necessary by the internal punctuation of clauses or listed items.)

1. When you arrive at school today, go and see the principal's secretary she has a letter for you.

2. Do not go back to the beginning if you make a mistake just keep going until you finish the job.

3. There was a variety of objects lying on the floor: old books, most of them with torn covers sheets of paper, thrown down by the clerks empty containers, which had obviously been used for paint and many empty shoeboxes.

4. After the party we returned to school, driving along the old highway, a dangerous road, luckily for us, we made it back safely.

5. In order to use the machine you should first remove the dust cover then press the green button, which starts the motor going then turn the speed control, at the top left, to the desired speed and, finally, adjust the heat control to the desired temperature.

6. The traveling circus transported many things, including large tents animals, safely secured in cages musical instruments of all types and costumes that were specially designed for each performer.

7. The film, which was very interesting, helped us to understand the special uses of magnetism, electricity, and heat and the presentation, as usual at such conferences, was followed by a general discussion.

Exercise 6.16: Semicolon

Necessary semicolons have been left out of the sentences. Insert them in the appropriate places.

1. On the cover of the catalog there were pictures of an electronic clock, selling for only $10 a steam iron, which cost $22.99 a gift-wrapped box, with no indication of what was inside it and a camera, complete with flash and leather carrying case.

2. A lot of money is spent on preserving our nation's water supply, which involves taking care of rivers, lakes, dams, and reservoirs but it remains a difficult task.

3. Everything went wrong yesterday: the children, who were late for school, started fighting my car, bought just a month earlier, would not start my best friend, recently recovered from a serious illness, called to say he was feeling sick again and my boss, a pleasant, kind man, told me that I might lose my job.

4. Our expert advisors can help your business grow call soon and ask for Ms. Fontaine or Mr. Legrand.

5. The first problem is that, in order to pay college fees, students must get loans, grants, or scholarships and the second problem is that they must study hard to pass the difficult exams.

Colon [*Handbook*, Section 6F, pages 218–20]

Exercise 6.17: Colon

Place colons in the appropriate places in the sentences.

1. They purchased many things after winning the lottery two new cars, a vacation home and a boat.

2. She read two long novels over her winter break *Anna Karenina* and *The Tale of Genji*.

3. Our class meets on Tuesdays at 9 45, not 8 45.

4. In the introduction to his famous book, *The Origin of the Species*, Charles Darwin begins

   When on board H.M.S. "Beagle," as a naturalist, I was much struck with certain facts in the distribution of the organic beings inhabiting South America, and in the geological relations of the present to the past inhabitants of that continent. These facts, as will be seen in the latter chapters of this volume, seemed to throw some light on the origin of the species—that mystery of mysteries, as it has been called by one of our greatest philosophers.

5. The young boy had the following in his pockets string, used chewing gum, pebbles, a catapult, some pennies, twigs, a broken pencil, and a few marbles.

6. The Japanese poet Basho once said "Do not seek to follow in the footsteps of the wise; seek what they sought."

7. Professor Jones began to write the recommendation letter for her best student, which began,

   To the Admissions Committee

   I am writing in support of Clara Morgan's application to your PhD program in Civil Engineering.

8. For this recipe, use a ratio of 31 (three to one)—three parts water and one part rice.

9. The odds against my horse winning are 52 (five to two).

10. As Ismael cleaned his room, he found the following items under the bed a dirty sock, two of his favorite comic books, and the homework assignment he could not find the night before.

11. To his surprise, Guiseppe found three English proverbs that referred to Rome "All roads lead to Rome," "Rome was not built in a day," and "When in Rome, do as the Romans do."

12. Leilani's daily work schedule is as follows check for mail, reply to urgent letters, attend meetings, have a business lunch, work with the planning department, and finally attend to mail orders.